This book is from:

_____

To you:

_____

Dedication

To my Son, Swahili, who is such a quiet and obedient child. He is very cooperative and does what he is asked to to do, even if he is not in the mood to do it.

Thank you for always listening and mastering the art of controlling your emotions.

It was a beautiful Saturday morning.
The sun was shining very bright outside
and peeking through the glass window.
The birds were chirping melodiously;
it almost sounded like they were singing a song.
Prince really did not feel like getting out of bed,
especially on the weekends.

Prince got very upset and lost his temper
when he was told to do something
that he did not want to do.
'Come on Prince,' mom said
as she slowly opened his bedroom door,
"it is time to get up,
let us begin this beautiful day."
'But mom',
Prince said
as he yanked the blanket off of his head.
'I don't want to!'
'You must brush your teeth
and change out of your pajamas
so that you can have breakfast',
mom said.

Prince jumped out of bed,
huffed and puffed,
stomped his feet,
and screamed,
'But mommy, I don't want to!'
'Come on, Prince,'
mom said calmly,
'Take a deep breath,
and calm yourself down.'

Prince closed his eyes,
breathed in and then out,
and sighed, 'Ooooookay,
I will brush my teeth
and change out of my pajamas.'

Prince really enjoyed breakfast,
but after he was done,
he had a few chores to do.
'Prince, come and pick up your toys.'

'Come on Prince,' mom said calmly,
'you must pick up after yourself.
Take a deep breath,
and calm yourself down.'
Prince closed his eyes,
breathed in and then out,
and sighed, 'Ooooookay,
I will put my toys away.'

Prince went outside
to play under his most favorite palm tree.
He brought his trains to play with this time.
They were red, yellow, blue and purple.
It was still sunny,
and the wind was blowing
the dry brown leaves in the air.
Prince could hear the sounds of the waves
splashing against the rocks.
Prince liked this time for play outside
before his Saturday afternoon
trips to the city with his mom.
Sometimes his new best friend
Peebo came over to play with him too.
Peebo lived across the street in a small blue house.

'Prince, it is time to get dressed to go to the city!
We must catch the next bus!
You know I cannot drive there; i
t is too crowded!'
Prince huffed and puffed,
stomped his feet, and screamed,
'But mommy, I don't want to!'
'Come on Prince,' mom said calmly,
'you must go and get dressed.'

'Come on Prince,' mom said calmly,
'you must go and get dressed.'
Prince closed his eyes,
breathed in and then out,
and sighed 'Ooooookay,
I will go and get dressed.'

Prince had a great time in the city with his mom.
They returned home with all kinds of fruits,
beans, and vegetables; oranges, bananas, cabbages,
chickpeas, lentils, and lots more.
It was now time for Prince
and his mom to have some fun,
fix dinner, wash the car, eat,
then off to their Saturday evening movie in the city.
Prince really liked this part of the day.
He liked to wash the car because it is blue,
and blue is his favorite color.
He also liked to help his mom to prepare dinner too.

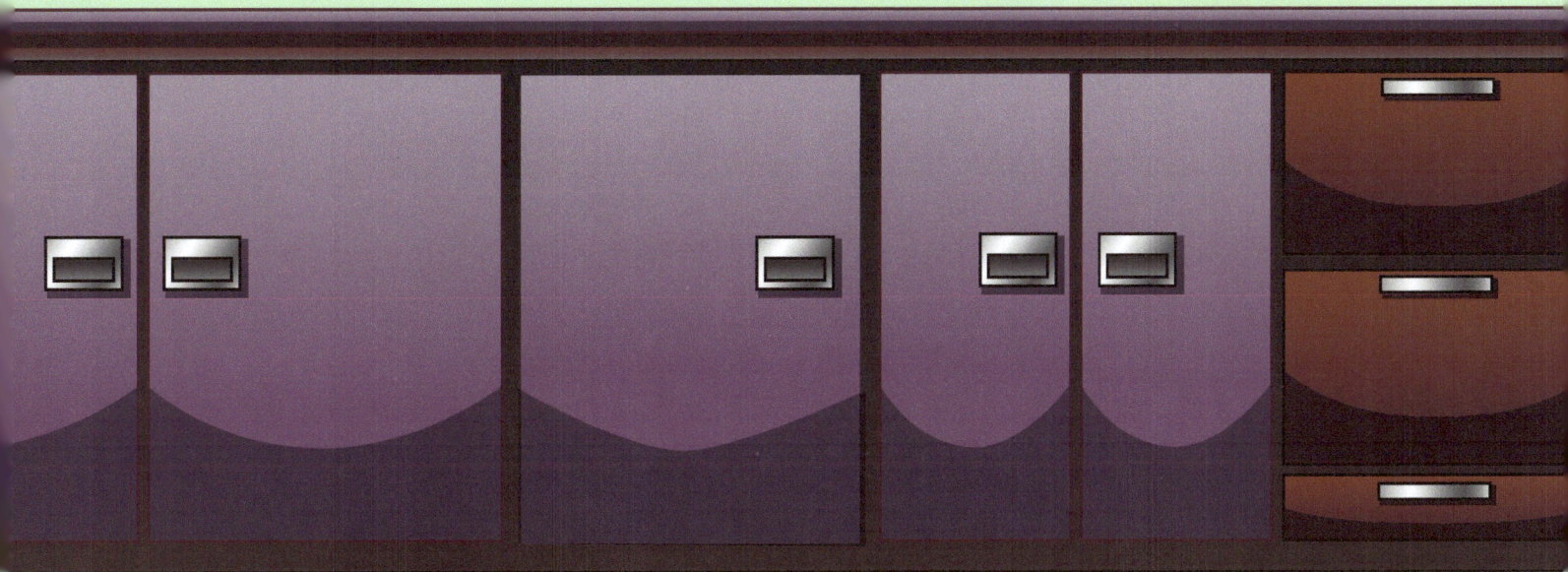

Prince and his mom had a wonderful time at the movie.
The movie was about a very calm boy
who was happy to help his mom to do chores around the house.
He was never angry.
He was always calm and smiled a lot.
'Mom', Prince said. 'That boy in the movie was very good.
He listened to his mom and did the things that she asked him to do.
I want to be like him, mom.'
'You can be Prince,' mom smiled.
'The things that I ask you to do
will help you to be a responsible adult when you grow up.'
'Responsible?' Prince questioned as he looked up at his mom.
'Yes, Prince. It means that you must do chores and care for people
every day as a part of your duty,' mom said.
'Duty?' Prince asked.
'Yes, Prince, duty is something that everyone has to do every day.'
'Oh!' Prince said happily.
'That means putting away my toys
and washing my hands are my responsibilities!
It is my duty to do them every day!'
'Yes, Prince!' Mom said with a big broad smile.
'You are correct!'

'As of tonight,
I will not frown and stomp my feet.
I will do what you ask me to do'.
Said Prince
'Now that is my Prince.
It is time to get ready for bed,
as we must wake up early
to go to the temple in the morning.
'I will mom.
I will! I will not frown and stomp my feet.
I will be a good boy as of tonight!
I will listen to you, mom!'
'Good Prince,' mom said.
'I am very happy that you have decided to change.'

She kissed him on his forehead,
said good night,
and turned out the lights.